MARTIN LUTHER KING JR.'S "I HAVE A DREAM"

FRONT SEAT OF HISTORY: FAMOUS SPEECHES

TAMRA ORR

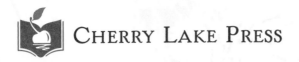

CHERRY LAKE PRESS

Published in the United States of America by Cherry Lake Publishing Group
Ann Arbor, Michigan
www.cherrylakepublishing.com

Reading Adviser: Marla Conn, MS, Ed., Literacy specialist, Read-Ability, Inc.
Content Adviser: Adam Fulton Johnson, PhD, Assistant Professor, History, Philosophy, and Sociology
   of Science, Michigan State University
Photo credits: © Ian Dagnall/Alamy Stock Photo, cover; © U.S. National Archives, 306-SSM-4D(80)10, 5;
   © Library of Congress, LC-DIG-ppmsca-37224, 6; © Library of Congress, LC-DIG-ds-04000, 8; © Library
   of Congress, LC-DIG-ds-00834, 9; © Library of Congress, LC-USZ62-133369, 10; © Library of Congress,
   LC-DIG-ppmsca-13245, 13; © Library of Congress, LC-USZ62-135695, 14; © Library of Congress,
   LC-DIG-ds-04413, 16; © Library of Congress, LC-DIG-ppmsca-03094, 19; © Library of Congress,
   LC-USZ62-116775, 20; © Library of Congress, LC-DIG-vrg-06860, 23; © Julie Clopper/Shutterstock.com,
   24; © Library of Congress, LC-USZ62-126558, 25; © Richard Cavalleri/Shutterstock.com, 26; © Library
   of Congress, LC-DIG-ds-04417, 28 [top]; © Library of Congress, LC-DIG-ds-00836, 28 [bottom]; ©
   Marian Weyo/Shutterstock.com, 29 [top]; © Library of Congress, LC-DIG-ppmsca-08102, 29 [bottom]

Cherry Lake Press is an imprint of Cherry Lake Publishing Group.

Library of Congress Cataloging-in-Publication Data
Names: Orr, Tamra, author.
Title: Martin Luther King Jr.'s "I have a dream" / Tamra Orr.
Description: Ann Arbor, Michigan : Cherry Lake Publishing, 2021 | Series: Front seat of history: famous
   speeches | Includes index. | Audience: Grades 4-6
Identifiers: LCCN 2020005674 (print) | LCCN 2020005675 (ebook) | ISBN 9781534168817 (hardcover) |
   ISBN 9781534170490 (paperback) | ISBN 9781534172333 (pdf) | ISBN 9781534174177 (ebook)
Subjects: LCSH: King, Martin Luther, Jr., 1929-1968. I have a dream—Juvenile literature. | King, Martin
   Luther, Jr., 1929-1968—Influence—Juvenile literature. | March on Washington for Jobs and Freedom
   (1963 : Washington, D.C.)—Juvenile literature. | Speeches, addresses, etc., American—Washington
   (D.C.)—Juvenile literature. | African Americans—Civil rights—History—20th century—Juvenile literature. |
   Civil rights movements—United States—History—20th century.
Classification: LCC E185.97.K5 O77 2021 (print) | LCC E185.97.K5 (ebook) | DDC 323.092—dc23
LC record available at https://lccn.loc.gov/2020005674
LC ebook record available at https://lccn.loc.gov/2020005675

Cherry Lake Publishing Group would like to acknowledge the work of the Partnership for 21st Century
Learning, a Network of Battelle for Kids. Please visit http://www.battelleforkids.org/networks/p21
for more information.

Printed in the United States of America
Corporate Graphics

ABOUT THE AUTHOR

Tamra Orr is the author of more than 500 nonfiction books for readers of all ages. A graduate
of Ball State University, she now lives in the Pacific Northwest with her family. When she isn't
writing books, she is either camping, reading or on the computer researching the latest topics.

TABLE OF CONTENTS

CHAPTER 1

The Chance of a Lifetime

In the early 1960s, the country was grappling with the issues of civil rights and racial equality. From **sit-ins** to **boycotts**, people could feel that change was coming. In 1963, Washington, DC, was selected as the site for the March on Washington for Jobs and Freedom. The march was designed to bring national attention to injustices and **discrimination** against African Americans. More than 250,000 people showed up, making it the largest gathering in the nation's history at that time. More than a dozen speakers and performers took the stage. But it was Dr. Martin Luther King Jr.'s speech that captured the audience's attention and made the civil rights leader a household name.

People traveled from all over the country to attend the March on Washington.

Two brothers made their way through Union Station in Washington, DC. At dawn, they boarded a bus to attend the March on Washington. They had finally arrived.

"Do you think lots of people will come?" Leon asked, looking around the station.

More than 2,000 buses full of people arrived in Washington, DC.

Before Jerome could answer, a bus pulled up and people began streaming out. It was followed by another bus—and then another and another. Soon, the station was overflowing.

"Does that answer your question?" Jerome replied.

"Let's get over to the Lincoln Memorial and find a good place to stand," suggested Jerome. "Maybe we can find some shade."

By the time the two of them got there, several thousand people were already waiting.

"All the shady spots are taken," Leon said with disappointment.

"Don't worry. I have a good second choice," said Jerome, leading his little brother over to the reflecting pool. The two grinned at each other. In seconds, their shoes and socks were off, their pant legs were pulled up, and their feet were in the water.

After the national anthem and a prayer, the first of the speakers began talking. The boys decided they were cooled off enough and rejoined the crowd. They were there to see Dr. Martin Luther King Jr. For the past week, their father had been telling them about everything King had been doing to help promote racial equality.

Many attendees held signs that demanded jobs, integrated schools, housing, and an end to racial discrimination.

"He's actually a Baptist minister," Mr. Hendriks had told his sons. "Even though he has gotten death threats, his home was bombed, and he has been stabbed and **assaulted**, Dr. King believes in nonviolence. He is an amazing man, and now you two will get the chance to see him in person." Mr. Hendriks shook his head sadly and said, "I wish I could go, but I can't miss work."

[21ST CENTURY SKILLS LIBRARY]

Temperatures reached 80 degrees Fahrenheit (27 degrees Celsius) on the day of the march; many people used the Reflecting Pool to cool off.

NATIONAL HEADQUARTERS

MARCH ON WASHINGTON FOR JOBS & FREEDOM

WED. AUG. 28

March on Washington organizers Bayard Rustin and Cleveland Robinson
stand outside headquarters in Harlem, New York.

Leon promised himself that he would try and remember every detail so he could share them with his father later.

By the middle of the afternoon, the two were sweaty and tired. But the speakers and singers made the boys excited and kept their energy high. Just then, they heard the words they'd been waiting for. "I have the pleasure to present to you, Dr. Martin Luther King." The place exploded in applause. This was the moment!

The Freedom Riders

*By the time King made his famous speech, the Freedom Riders had been taking buses across the country for several years. Both black and white activists rode these buses throughout the American South to protest **segregated** bus terminals. They would get off the buses and go into the "whites only" restaurants and restrooms. This often resulted in hostility and even violence. A number of Freedom Riders were beaten, and their buses were even firebombed. Finally, Attorney General Robert Kennedy provided protection for the Riders by sending in the National Guard. The Riders achieved their goal. In November 1961, segregation on interstate buses was declared illegal.*

CHAPTER 2

"We Will Not Be Satisfied"

The crowd roared as Martin Luther King Jr. walked up to the **podium**. "I am happy to join with you today in what will go down in history as the greatest demonstration for freedom in the history of our nation," he began. King then proceeded to speak about how President Abraham Lincoln's **Emancipation** Proclamation was "a great beacon light of hope" to so many. However, he pointed out, 100 years later African Americans still struggled with segregation and discrimination.

Leon thought of his father. All around him, people were cheering in agreement.

King compared the promise of "life, liberty, and the pursuit of happiness"—words written long ago by the nation's Founding

Despite fighting for freedom in Europe in World War II, African American veterans came home to a segregated country.

In 1965, King and other activists marched from Selma to Montgomery, Alabama, to demand fair voting rights for African Americans.

Fathers—to a bad check. "A check which has come back marked 'insufficient funds,'" he explained.

As people clapped and cheered, Leon leaned over to Jerome and whispered, "What's 'insufficient funds' supposed to mean?"

"Beats me," Jerome answered, shrugging.

"There will be neither rest nor tranquility in America until the Negro is granted his citizenship rights," King continued. "The whirlwinds of revolt will continue to shake the foundations of our nation until the bright day of justice emerges."

King was quick to add that revolt was not to be violent. "In the process of gaining our rightful place, we must not be guilty of wrongful deeds," he explained. He directly encouraged the thousands of people listening to him in person—or on one of the three television networks broadcasting his speech—to struggle with "dignity and discipline."

"Again and again, we must rise to the majestic heights of meeting physical force with soul force," he said.

"Dad will like that one," Jerome whispered.

President John F. Kennedy met with civil rights leaders
after the March on Washington.

Next, King turned to the question that Leon had heard some
people at school discussing: When will black people be satisfied?
King made it clear that many changes were needed before people
could rest. "We can never be satisfied as long as our bodies, heavy
with the fatigue of travel, cannot gain lodging in the motels of

the highways and the hotels of the cities," he said. "We can never be satisfied as long as our children are stripped of their self-hood and robbed of their dignity by signs stating 'For Whites Only.' We cannot be satisfied as long as a Negro in Mississippi cannot vote and a Negro in New York believes he has nothing for which to vote. We will not be satisfied until 'justice rolls down like waters and righteousness like a mighty stream.'"

The 1964 Civil Rights Act

When President John F. Kennedy pushed the idea of a Civil Rights Act, he ran into a lot of opposition. The law was written to end segregation in all public places and ban employment discrimination based on race, color, religion, sex, or national origin. But many southern congressmen fought against the act. After Kennedy was **assassinated**, *Vice President Lyndon B. Johnson became president and continued the fight for the Civil Rights Act. It was signed into law on July 2, 1964. It helped to inspire additional civil rights legislation, such as the Voting Rights Act the following year.*

CHAPTER 3

Sharing a Dream

Martin Luther King Jr. paused for a few seconds. Suddenly, a voice from behind him rang out. "Tell them about the dream, Martin. Tell them about the dream." King glanced toward his friend and then pushed his notes aside.

"Watch this," whispered Jerome. "You've been listening to a speaker. Now you're going to hear a Baptist preacher."

"Let us not wallow in the valley of despair, I say to you today, my friends. And so even though we face the difficulties of today and tomorrow, I still have a dream," King began. He described these dreams to an eager audience, often pausing as the applause grew. He talked about his dream of "the sons of former slaves and the sons of slave owners" sitting down together "at the table of

In 1957, a little boy watches as a mob gathers to protest the admission of the Little Rock Nine into an all-white school in Tennessee.

brotherhood." Over and over, King spoke of his dreams of freedom, equality, and justice for everyone, including his own family. "I have a dream that my four little children will one day live in a nation where they will not be judged by the color of their skin but by the content of their character," he stated.

Leon felt goosebumps rush down both arms when he heard this. For the first time, he believed that real change was possible—and that he was here to see it begin.

Coretta Scott King was also extremely active in the civil rights movement and continued to be even after her husband's death.

King shifted from speaking about dreams to hopes. He hoped that the nation would transform "into a beautiful symphony of brotherhood." He quoted the patriotic song "My Country 'Tis of Thee" and cried out for freedom to ring all over the country, including in the southern states that were most resistant to accepting equality.

Then, King stood up straighter and raised his right hand. "And when this happens, and when we allow freedom to ring, when we let it ring from every village and every hamlet, from every state and every city, we will be able to speed up that day when all of God's children, black men and white men . . . will be able to join hands and sing in the words of the old **Negro spiritual**: 'Free at last! Free at last! Thank God Almighty, we are free at last!'"

King's last words were met with thunderous applause and cheering. There were many cries of "Amen!" Everyone, including Leon and Jerome, was up on their feet, shouting and waving their hands, the afternoon's heat forgotten.

A Fatal Shot

King was assassinated on April 4, 1968, as he stood on a balcony at the Lorraine Motel in Memphis, Tennessee. James Earl Ray was spotted at the scene, and his fingerprints were found on the gun. Ray was arrested 2 months later at Heathrow Airport in London. He pleaded guilty to murder and was sentenced to 99 years in prison.

"Free at Last" —Or Soon

Leon carefully shifted in his chair while Pete worked his magic with his clipper. He had been coming to Pete's Barbershop since he moved to Chicago in 1989. Chatting with Pete was one of the best parts of these visits. Over the years, the two men had discussed everything from family and work to politics and news.

"Oh, by the way," Pete said as he finished clipping Leon's hair. "We need to move your appointment next month. It was scheduled for Martin Luther King Jr. Day by mistake, and we will be closed."

"Really?" Leon asked in surprise.

King continues to be a cultural icon, with depictions
in artwork across the world.

"We do it every year," explained Pete. "It is our way of paying
respect to one of the most amazing civil rights leaders in the world."

Leon smiled. "Jerome and I were there in Washington when
Dr. King gave his famous speech," he admitted softly. "I don't think
I ever told you."

Pete froze, his hands in midair over Leon's hair. "What?" he asked
in shock. "Are you kidding?"

The Martin Luther King Jr. Memorial opened in 2011 in Washington, DC.

Leon shook his head. "It was a very **humid** afternoon," he said, "Jerome and I spent the beginning part of the day with our feet dangling in the reflecting pool by the Lincoln Memorial."

The room had gone silent. Leon looked around and realized everyone was listening.

"Dr. King was the last speaker of the day," he said. "Did you know, the last 6 minutes that helped him become so famous, he just **ad-libbed**?" Leon chuckled. "Thanks to all of the television

King received the Nobel Peace Prize in 1964, honoring his work in the civil rights movement.

I HAVE A DREAM
MARTIN LUTHER KING, JR.
THE MARCH ON WASHINGTON
FOR JOBS AND FREEDOM
AUGUST 28, 1963

The words of King's speech were added to the steps
he stood on at the Lincoln Memorial.

coverage, soon the entire world knew the message of justice and peace that he was sharing. He changed my life."

"Is that the reason you became a judge?" Pete asked.

"Well, first I started out as a lawyer," Leon said. "I specialized in cases of discrimination and racial injustice. I wanted to help create that 'beautiful symphony of brotherhood' that Dr. King spoke about."

"Think we're any closer to that than we were then?" asked Pete.

"I do," said Leon. "Not nearly as close as I'm sure he thought we would be, but we are closer." He nodded to the other men in the shop. "'Free at last,' or at least soon."

Around the World

Today, more than half a century since King told the world about his dream, his speech has been voted one of the greatest in all of American history. His words are echoed across the world as many people fight injustice within their own communities. Originally inspired by the teachings of Mahatma Gandhi, King's nonviolent approach has influenced generations of civil rights protesters.

1963

The March for Jobs and Freedom is held in Washington, DC, where Martin Luther King Jr. gives his "I Have a Dream" speech.

1965

King joins the voting rights march from Selma to Montgomery, Alabama; the Voting Rights Act passes.

1960

1965

1970

1964

The Civil Rights Act passes; King receives the Nobel Peace Prize.

1968

King is assassinated on April 4.

1983
Martin Luther King Jr. Day is adopted as a federal holiday.

1975

1980

1985

1980
Martin Luther King Jr. National Historic Site is established in Atlanta, Georgia.

Speech Highlight

"Even though we face the difficulties of today and tomorrow, I still have a dream. It is a dream deeply rooted in the American dream. I have a dream that one day this nation will rise up and live out the true meaning of its creed, 'We hold these truths to be self-evident, that all men are created equal.' I have a dream that one day on the red hills of Georgia, the sons of former slaves and the sons of former slave owners will be able to sit down together at the table of brotherhood. I have a dream that one day even the state of Mississippi, a state sweltering with the heat of injustice, sweltering with the heat of oppression, will be transformed into an oasis of freedom and justice. I have a dream that my four little children will one day live in a nation where they will not be judged by the color of their skin but by the content of their character. I have a dream today."

Read the full speech at https://kinginstitute.stanford.edu/king-papers/documents/i-have-dream-address-delivered-march-washington-jobs-and-freedom.

Research and Act

There are many different techniques used in speeches to make them more powerful and more memorable. What type of technique is used depends on the speech's length, message, and style of the speaker.

Research

Research and find present-day activists, locations, or monuments that use words or phrases from Martin Luther King Jr.'s "I Have a Dream" speech. How do they use them? Are they successful? What is their message or goal? Write two to three paragraphs.

Act

Do you have a dream? Write down a list of five things that would make the world a better place. Then take action. Research ways to give back to your community. Volunteer at a food bank, library, or park.

Further Reading

Outcalt, Todd. *All About Martin Luther King, Jr.* Indianapolis, IN: Blue River Press, 2016.

Ruiz, Rachel. *Martin Luther King Jr.: A Graphic History of America's Great Civil Rights Leader.* Hauppauge, NY: B.E.S. Pub. Co., 2019.

Susienka, Kristen. *Martin Luther King Jr.* New York, NY: PowerKids Press, 2020.

Wittenstein, Barry. *A Place to Land: Martin Luther King Jr. and the Speech That Inspired a Nation.* New York, NY: Holiday House, 2019.

GLOSSARY

ad-libbed (AD LIBD) spoke in front of a crowd without preparing for it

assassinated (uh-SAS-uh-nay-tid) murdered for political reasons

assaulted (uh-SAWL-tid) physically attacked

boycotts (BOI-kahts) refusals to do business with companies as a protest, in hopes of bringing about a change

discrimination (dis-krim-ih-NAY-shuhn) unfair behavior toward others based on differences in things such as race, age, or gender

emancipation (ih-man-suh-PAY-shuhn) freedom

humid (HYOO-mid) high level of moisture in the air

Negro spiritual (NEE-groh SPIR-ih-choo-uhl) a song sung by African American slaves

podium (POH-dee-uhm) a stand with a surface for holding papers, for use by a person giving a speech

segregated (SEG-rih-gay-tid) describing places that kept certain people or groups apart by race

sit-ins (SIT-inz) protests where people come into a business and sit, without leaving

INDEX